www.booksbyboxer.com

Bee Three Publishing is an imprint of Books By Boxer
Published by
Books By Boxer, Leeds, LS13 4BS UK
Books by Boxer (EU), Dublin D02 P593 IRELAND
© Books By Boxer 2023
All Rights Reserved
MADE IN CHINA
ISBN: 9781915410306

AIR YOU READY TO GROW?

POTHOS

ZANZIBAR GEM

SPIDER PLANT

HELP TO DETOXIFY YOUR AIR AND MAKE YOUR
HOME A CLEANER SPACE WITH THESE
AIR PURIFYING PLANTS!

ENGLISH IVY

ARECA PALM

PEACE LILY

KEEP YOUR FURRY FRIENDS SAFE!

CHINESE MONEY PLANT

ORCHID

RATTLESNAKE

EVEN IF YOU CAN'T LOOK AFTER YOUR PLANTS, THE LEAST YOU CAN DO IS LOOK AFTER YOUR FOUR-LEGGED FAMILY WITH THESE PET-SAFE PLANTS!

COCONUT PALM

BOSTON FERN

VENUS FLYTRAP

SHUT THE BLINDS!

LUCKY BAMBOO

CHINESE EVERGREEN

CALATHEA

CHOOSE THE RIGHT PLANTS THAT WILL THRIVE IN YOUR HOBBIT HOLE! THESE PLANTS ARE THE PERFECT BOTANICAL BUDDIES THAT THRIVE WITH NO SUNLIGHT!

CAST IRON

SNAKE PLANT

MONSTERA

STURDY STEMS & RESILIENT ROOTS

AIR PLANT

STRING OF PEARLS

JADE PLANT

THESE PLANTS ARE VERY HARD TO KILL, THANKS TO THEIR ROBUSTNESS AND ADAPTABILITY, PERFECT FOR PEOPLE WHO HAVE A HISTORY OF PLANT NEGLECT!

MADAGASCAR DRAGON TREE

SNAKE PLANT

ALOE VERA

ASTROLOGICAL AGRICULTURE

ARIES
ZEBRA HAWORTHIA

TAURUS
FIDDLE LEAF FIG

GEMINI
ENGLISH IVY

CANCER
PEACE LILY

LEO
BROMELIAD

VIRGO
BRAIDED MONEY TREE

WHETHER YOU NEED A PLANT THAT MATCHES YOUR DOTING PERSONALITY, OR ONE THAT IS JUST AS INDEPENDENT AS YOU — FIND YOUR MATCH HERE!

LIBRA
STRING OF PEARLS

SCORPIO
SNAKE PLANT

SAGITTARIUS
MARANTA PLANT

CAPRICORN
JADE PLANT

AQUARIUS
ZZ PLANT

PISCES
SPIDER PLANT

DOZY DECOR

PEACE LILY

LAVENDER

ENGLISH IVY

DID YOU KNOW THAT SOME PLANTS ARE ACTUALLY GREAT AT HELPING YOU RELAX? POP THESE IN YOUR BEDROOM TO HELP MAKE YOU UNWIND AND DOZE MORE DEEPLY!

ARECA PALM

SNAKE PLANT

JASMINE

ALLERGIES SUCC!

BAMBOO PALM

THE LADY PALM

MADAGASCAR DRAGON TREE

IF YOU'RE ALLERGY PRONE, SOME INDOOR FOLIAGE COULD BE YOUR WORST NIGHTMARE! THESE PLANT PALS ARE FRIENDLY TO YOUR ALLERGIES — NO NEED TO FEEL LEFT OUT ANY LONGER!

PEACE LILY

ARECA PLANT

SNAKE PLANT

BOTANIC BATHROOMS

BOSTON FERN

ALOCASIA

AIR PLANT

THESE PLANTS ARE GREAT TO ADD A POP OF COLOR TO YOUR BATHROOM! THEY CAN HELP CREATE YOUR OWN LITTLE OASIS — GREAT FOR BRINGING A TROPICAL VIBE INTO YOUR HOME!

ALOE VERA

GOLDEN POTHOS

HEART-LEAF PHILODENDRON

COMMON CACTI

BARREL CACTUS

THESE SPIKY BALLS CAN BE MINIATURE, BUT HAVE POTENTIAL TO GROW UP TO 3 FEET TALL!

BISHOP'S CAP CACTUS

NATIVE TO MEXICO, THIS CACTUS LOOKS LIKE A PIECE C CONTEMPORARY ART.

LADY FINGER CACTUS

IT'S STEMS RESEMBLE FINGERS HENCE IT'S NAME, AND CAN REACH THE LENGTH OF 8 INCHES.

SAGUARO CACTUS

THIS ICONIC SPECIES OF CACTI CAN BE FOUND IN EVERY CARTOON DESERT...

IF YOU'RE JUST STARTING OUT ON YOUR PLANT-OWNING ADVENTURE, THEN A CACTUS IS AN EASY WIN. HERE ARE 8 COMMON CACTI:

MOON CACTUS

A GLOWING RED MUTANT THAT MUST BE GROWN AND GRAFTED ONTO A NORMAL CACTUS BECAUSE IT LACKS CHLOROPHYLL!

BUNNY EAR CACTUS

THIS FUN CACTUS RESEMBLES BUNNY EARS AND ITS HAIR-LIKE SPINES LOOK LIKE FUR!

BLUE COLUMNAR CACTUS

THIS IS SO VIBRANT AND BLUE THAT YOU ALMOST WON'T BELIEVE THEY'RE REAL. THEY OFTEN HAVE CONTRASTING ORANGE SPINES, MAKING THEM LOOK EVEN MORE BEAUTIFUL AND UNREAL!

CHRISTMAS CACTUS

SO CALLED BECAUSE THEY FLOWER FROM LATE NOVEMBER TO LATE JANUARY, THIS PLANT DOESN'T LOOK LIKE YOUR TYPICAL CACTUS!

" *Plants*
GIVE US
Oxygen
FOR THE
Lungs
AND FOR THE
Soul. "

- Terri Guillemets

SUNS & SPIKES

YOUR CACTI LOVES THE WARMTH, BUT THAT DOESN'T MEAN A WINDOWSILL IS THE BEST LOCATION FOR YOUR PRICKLY PLANTS...

CACTI SURVIVE AND THRIVE THE MOST WHEN THEY HAVE A GOOD SOURCE OF LIGHT.

TOO LITTLE SUN CAN MAKE YOUR CACTUS STRESSED AND IT MIGHT START LOOKING A LITTLE PALE!

IF YOUR CACTUS BEGINS TO TURN BROWN OR YELLOW IN PLACES, IT MIGHT BE GETTING SUNBURNED FROM TOO MUCH SUN EXPOSURE.

PLACE YOUR CACTI IN THE SHADE ON AN EVENING TO PROTECT IT FROM THE STRONG EVENING SUN.

HOME YOUR CACTUS IN A BRIGHTLY LIT ROOM, BUT NOT IN DIRECT SUNLIGHT - IT'LL GET A TAN!

DESERTLY DRENCHED

THINK YOUR CACTI DON'T NEED WATERING?
BAD NEWS MY FRIEND, IT'S A MYTH!

WATER YOUR CACTI ONCE A
WEEK IN THE SUMMER, BUT ONLY
ONCE A MONTH IN WINTER.

YOUR CACTUS WILL GO
'DORMANT' IN WINTER,
MEANING IT WILL
PAUSE ITS GROWTH.

SMALL, BABY CACTI NEED
MORE WATER (TO GROW BIG AND
STRONG), BUT OLDER CACTI SHOULD
BE WATERED LESS FREQUENTLY.

ONLY WATER YOUR CACTI
WHEN THE SOIL IS COMPLETELY
DRY, OTHERWISE YOU RISK
OVERWATERING THEM.

RELOCATION, RELOCATION

SO YOU WANT TO RELOCATE YOUR CACTUS. WHAT NOW? IT'S NOT AS EASY AS JUST POPPING YOUR SPIKY FRIEND INTO A NEW POT , BUT YOU CAN FOLLOW THESE STEPS TO ENSURE YOUR CACTUS STAYS HAPPY AND ON POINT!

CHOOSE A NEW LOCATION.

PICK A POT - CACTI LIKE TERRACOTTA POTS THE BEST BECAUSE THEY HELP ABSORB EXTRA MOISTURE.

FIND SOME IDEAL WELL-DRAINING SOIL - REGULAR SOIL IS NO GOOD FOR CACTI AS THE ORGANIC MATERIALS CAN RETAIN WATER AND CAUSE ROOT ROT.

ADD YOUR SOIL TO 1/3 OF THE POT, POP YOUR CACTUS INTO ITS NEW HOME.

FILL THE REMAINING SPACE WITH SOIL AND PRESS THE SOIL DOWN GENTLY.

GIVE YOUR CACTUS A DRINK - A JOB WELL DONE!

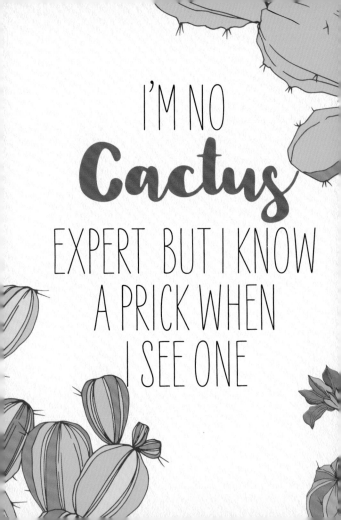

IN A PRICKLE

IF YOU'RE NOT SURE IF YOUR CACTUS IS STILL BREATHING,
THEN HERE ARE SOME TELL-TALE SIGNS YOUR CACTUS
HAS KICKED THE POT...

IT'S ALL SHRIVELLED UP.

IT HAS BROWN,
DISCOLOURED PATCHES.

IT'S GONE SOFT AND MUSHY.

IT'S LOOSE AND WOBBLY
IN ITS SOIL (IT MAY
EVEN FALL OVER)

IT SMELLS DEAD.

IF YOU TRULY THINK YOUR CACTUS IS
DEAD, THEN I'M SORRY TO SAY, YOU'RE
PROBABLY RIGHT. WHY NOT ADD IT TO
A COMPOST HEAP, AND IT CAN HELP
ANOTHER PLANT ONE DAY?

25

YOU'RE POTTY!

YOU CAN'T LET YOUR CACTUS LIVE ITS LIFE IN A SHABBY, SMALL, PLASTIC POT AND EXPECT IT TO THRIVE LIKE THE CACTUS IT WANTS TO BE. HELP YOUR BUDDING PLANT LOOK SHARP WITH THIS NEAT TERRARIUM GUIDE!

GLASS TERRARIUM

GLASS TERRARIUMS ARE A FUN WAY TO DISPLAY YOUR PRICKLY PLANTS, HERE'S HOW TO BUILD YOUR OWN:

1. CHOOSE A GLASS CONTAINER (ONE WITHOUT A LID!)

2. FILL THE BOTTOM WITH A LAYER OF GRAVEL AND ROCKS.

3. ADD A LAYER OF MESH (TO KEEP A GOOD STRUCTURE

4. ADD CACTI-FRIENDLY SOIL ON TOP.

5. POP YOUR CACTI INTO THE SOIL.

6. PLACE A THIN LAYER OF SAND ON TOP OF THE SOIL AND ADD YOUR FAVOURITE ROCKS!

TIPS & PRICKS

THOUGH RESILIENT AND FAIRLY SIMPLE TO CARE FOR, THERE ARE SOME THINGS THAT CAN GO WRONG WHEN IT COMES TO LOOKING AFTER YOUR EASY-GOING CACTI...

TREATING ALL CACTI THE SAME

LIKE PEOPLE, CACTI COME FROM ALL WALKS OF LIFE. ONE CACTI'S LITTLE IS ANOTHER CACTI'S LOT, SO MONITOR YOUR PRICKLY PLANT TO FIND OUT ITS HAPPY MEDIUM.

TOO WET OR TOO WILTED

CACTI ARE COOL LITTLE CREATURES WHO STORE WATER IN THEIR STEMS! YOU DON'T NEED TO WATER THEM EVERY DAY, BUT REMEMBER THAT THEY STILL NEED AN OCCASIONAL TRICKLE.

SHINE A LITTLE LIGHT

BOTH TOO MUCH AND TOO LITTLE SUNLIGHT CAN LEAVE YOUR CACTI FEELING SORRY FOR ITSELF. OPEN THE BLINDS BUT KEEP YOUR CACTUS AT A SAFE DISTANCE FROM THE SUN'S RAYS TO ENSURE A HAPPY PLANT.

HAPPY HOME, HAPPY CACTI

IF YOUR CACTUS IS POTTED IN A CHEAP, SMALL PLANT POT WITH SOME HEAVY SOIL, THEN CHANCES ARE, YOUR CACTUS ISN'T HAVING A GOOD TIME. GET IT RE-POTTED!

DON'T BUG ME

YOU WANT TO KEEP YOUR CACTI SAFE FROM PESTS, BUT USING HARMFUL PESTICIDES ON YOUR PRECIOUS PLANTS WILL ONLY CAUSE YOU TROUBLE. MOST CACTI ACTUALLY DETER BUGS.

"*Like*
PEOPLE,
Plants
RESPOND TO
EXTRA
Attention."

- H. PETER LOEWER

SUCC THESE TIPS

DO YOU KNOW HOW TO CARE FOR THE LITTLE SUCC-ERS? THESE QUICK TIPS WILL KEEP YOUR PLANT BABIES THRIVING!

PICK A SUCCULENT THAT WILL STAND A CHANCE!

ONLY WATER WHEN THE SOIL FEELS DRY - AND DRAIN EXCESS WATER!

WELL DRAINING SOIL WORKS BEST - SUCCULENTS LIKE TO STAY DRY.

SUCCULENTS ARE HAPPY IN ALMOST ANY CONTAINER THAT HAS A DRAINAGE HOLE.

MOST SUCCULENTS LOVE LIGHT!

REMOVE ANY DYING LEAVES TO KEEP YOUR SUCCULENTS LOOKING WELL!

SNIP AND TRIPLE!

OFF WITH YOUR HEA

USING SCISSORS, SNIP A 3
INCH LONG SECTION
OF YOUR PLANT.

PLUCKER UP

INDIVIDUAL LEAVES ARE ANOTHER
GREAT WAY TO TURN ONE PLANT
INTO TWO. JUST HOLD THE LEAF
CLOSE TO THE STEM, AND EASE IT
OFF EASILY BY TWISTING!

READY TO GROW

PLACE YOUR SNIPPETS INTO
A DISH FILLED WITH FAST-
DRAINING SOIL, AND LEAVE
FOR AROUND 3 DAYS.

SO YOU'VE GOT YOUR SUCCULENT AND YOU WANT
TO USE SIMPLE MATHS TO TURN ONE SUCC INTO TWO.
IT'S NOT ROCKET SCIENCE, JUST FOLLOW
THESE EASY STEPS!

WET & WAIT

AFTER 3 DAYS, USE A SPRAY BOTTLE
TO SQUIRT THE PLANT UNTIL
THE SOIL IS MOIST (NOT SOAKED).
REPEAT WHENEVER THE SOIL DRIES.

HERE WE GO

AROUND SIX TO SEVEN WEEKS
AFTER THE SNIP, YOU'LL NOTICE
TINY LEAVES EMERGING. YOUR
PARENT SNIPPET MIGHT LOOK
SHRIVELLED - THIS IS DUE TO IT
FEEDING THE BABY LEAVES.

PATIENCE... IN ABOUT THREE TO
FOUR WEEKS, ROOTS WILL SPROUT!

31

STANDARD SUCCULENTS

CALIFORNIA SUNSET

THIS REDDISH-COLORED ROSETTE SUCCULENT WITH VERY THICK LEAVES GROWS WELL. THE COMPACT ROSETTES ARE SIMILAR TO ECHEVERIA.

HENS & CHICKS

WITH HERBAL USES, THIS SUCC CAN HELP TREAT MANY THINGS LIKE SUNBURN AND DIARRHOEA!

ROSEUM

THEY HAVE BRIGHT GREEN SCALLOPED LEAVES AND PALE PINK FLOWERS SHAPED LIKE STARS. THIS PLANT ADDS A HINT OF COLOR TO ANY BORING WINDOWSILL!

ZEBRA HAWORTHIA

RESEMBLES MINI ALOE PLANTS WITH ROSETTES OF FLESHY GREEN LEAVES GENEROUSLY COVERED WITH WHITE PEARLY WARTS OR BANDS.

IF YOU'RE CONSIDERING OWNING A SUCCULENT, THEN YOU SHOULD KNOW THE MOST COMMON TYPES!

JELLY BEAN

COLORFUL CHUBBY, LITTLE RED-TIPPED LEAVES THAT LOOK LIKE JELLY BEANS MAKE IT A FAVORITE GO TO HOUSE PLANT.

PERLE VON NURNBERG

WONDERFULLY DECORATIVE EVERGREEN SUCCULENT WITH FLESHY, OBOVATE LEAVES GROWING AS A ROSETTE.

LAVENDER SCALLOP

THESE ARE CALLED 'LAVENDER SCALLOPS' FROM THE SHAPE AND COLOR OF ITS LEAVES. IT HAS FEW PESTS.

DEBBIE

AN ECHEVERIA HYBRID SUCCULENT. IT HAS BLUISH-PURPLE LEAVES THAT DEVELOP PINK TIPS WHEN THE PLANT IS UNDER HEALTHY STRESS.

33

SOAKING SUCCS

SUCCULENTS MIGHT BE MOSTLY SELF-SUFFICIENT, BUT THAT DOESN'T MEAN YOU'RE ALLOWED TO SUCK AT WATERING THEM.

1. WATER YOUR SUCCS EVERY 2-3 WEEKS IN THE SUMMER AND ONCE A MONTH IN WINTER

2. MAKE SURE YOUR SOIL IS DRY BEFORE RE-WATERING (SUCCS STORE WATER IN THEIR LEAVES)

3. SELECT POTS WITH DRAINAGE HOLES, AS TOO MUCH EXCESS WATER CAN CAUSE ROOT ROT!

4. USE FAST-DRAINING SOIL FOR GOOD DRAINAGE, IT'LL STOP YOUR PLANT GETTING WATER LOGGED!

5. MONITOR THE TEMPERATUR AND WATER YOUR PLANT LESS WHEN IT'S COLDER.

DON'T SUCC TOO BADLY

YOU SHOULD KNOW THAT IT'S NOT ALWAYS POSSIBLE TO PROTECT YOUR PLANTS. THINGS CAN GO WRONG, THOUGH MOST CAN BE PREDICTED AND SOLVED...

NOT DRAINING YOUR SUCCS

A PLANT POT WITHOUT DRAINAGE IS LIKE YOU SITTING IN A BATH ALL DAY. WE GO WRINKLY, YOUR SUCCULENTS GET ROOT ROT.

MISTING FOR MOISTURE

YOUR SUCCULENTS NEED WATER AND MISTING MOST SUCCS WILL DO NOTHING BUT MAKE YOU LOOK CLUELESS. JUST STOP.

NOT WATERING ENOUGH

YOUR SUCCS ARE VERY SELF-SUFFICIENT, BUT THEY STILL NEED WATER! DON'T DEHYDRATE THE POOR THING, GIVE IT A DRINK!

LET IT SHINE

AS LONG AS YOU DON'T PUT IT IN THE GLARING SUN, YOUR SUCC WILL LOVE YOU FOR PLACING IT IN A WELL-LIT SPACE.

CROWDED POT

YOUR SUCCULENTS DON'T WANT TO LOOK LIKE SARDINES IN A TIN - SPACE THEM OUT, AND FOR THE LOVE OF ALL THINGS PLANTY, DON'T MIX THEM WITH NON-SUCCULENTS.

"MY GREEN
thumb
CAME ONLY AS
A RESULT OF THE

mistakes

I MADE WHILE
LEARNING TO SEE
THINGS FROM THE

plant's

POINT OF VIEW."

- H. Fred Dale

IT'S NOT POT LUCK

IS YOUR SUCCULENT LOOKING TOO SMALL FOR ITS POT? YOU'LL NEED TO BUY IT A NEW HOME AND FIND A COSY NEW SPOT!

FIND A CLASSY NEW POT FOR YOUR SUCCULENT!

GENTLY LIFT THE SUCC OUT OF ITS OLD POT - YOU MAY WANT TO TWIST AS YOU PULL TO MAKE IT EASIER.

SEPARATE YOUR SUCCULENT'S ROOTS A LITTLE BY POKING THE SOIL. THIS IS TO HELP YOUR PLANT GROW WELL IN ITS NEW POT.

USING A FAST DRAINING SOIL MIX (SUCH AS CACTUS MIX), FILL YOUR NEW POT HALFWAY.

POP YOUR LITTLE SUCCULENT INTO ITS NEW HOME AND COVER THE ROOTS ENTIRELY WITH SOIL.

PRESS THE SOIL DOWN GENTLY.

WAIT ONE WEEK BEFORE REWARDING YOUR SUCCULENT WITH A DRINK.

WELL THAT SUCCS

HAVE YOU NOTICED YOUR SUCCULENT LOOKING A LITTLE DOWN IN THE DUMPS LATELY? HERE ARE A FEW INDICATIONS THAT YOUR CUTE LITTLE HOUSEPLANT IS ON ITS WAY TO HOUSEPLANT HEAVEN:

IT'S ALL SHRIVELLED UP.

ITS LEAVES ARE TURNING BLACK OR RED.

IT HAS BROWN SPOTS OR MUSHY LEAVES.

THE LEAVES WILL BEGIN TO DROOP.

IT LOOKS VERY 'LANKY'.

IT OFFICIALLY LOOKS LIKE IT'S DIED.

SO YOUR SUCCULENT HAS SAID ITS GOODBYES AND NOW YOU'RE LEFT WI' DEAD PLANT. POP IT INTO A COMPOS HEAP, AND IT MIGHT BRING LIFE TO ANOTHER PLANT ONE DAY!

VERA MANY USES

A MEDICINAL PLANT, THIS SUCCULENT HAS BEEN USED FOR THOUSANDS OF YEARS TO TREAT MANY AILMENTS, FROM BURNS TO CONSTIPATION! BUT WHAT IS THIS MAGNIFICENT PLANT USED FOR TODAY? HERE'S JUST SOME OF ITS MODERN USES:

HEALS & SOOTHES
WHETHER IT'S SUNBURN, BURNS, CUTS AND SCRAPES, ALOE IS THE BEST.

ORAL HEALTH
WASHING ONE'S MOUTH WITH ALOE JUICE SEVERAL TIMES A DAY CAN HEAL STUBBORN INFECTIONS.

IMMUNITY BOOSTER
ALOE VERA IS A GREAT HELP IN KEEPING YOUR IMMUNE SYSTEM AT ITS PEAK.

RASHES & ALLERGIC REACTIONS
IF YOU HAVE A SORE BOTTOM, ALOE VERA IS HERE TO KISS IT BETTER.

ACHES & PAINS
ALOE VERA IS A NATURAL ANTI-INFLAMMATORY, SO RUB IT INTO YOUR ACHES & PAINS!

ACNE
FOUND IN MANY FACE WASHES AND MASKS, ALOE IS A GREAT ACNE BANISHER.

POT IT OVER *VERA*

ALOE VERA IS A SPECIAL SUCCULENT, SO IT SHOULD HAVE ITS VERY OWN POT - ONLY THE BEST FOR OUR VERA!

TERRACOTTA OR CERAMIC

A TERRACOTTA OR CERAMIC POT IS HANDY FOR SUCCULENTS THAT DON'T REQUIRE A LOT OF WATER. DUE TO THEIR BREATHABLE PROPERTIES, YOU CAN ENSURE YOUR LIFESAVING ALOE DOESN'T GET WATERLOGGED!

THE PERFECT SIZED POT SHOULD BE 2-INCHES LARGER THAN THE SUCCULENT'S CURRENT SIZE.

ENSURE YOUR POT HAS A DRAINAGE HOLE TO ALLOW EXCESS WATER TO DRAIN - ALOE ISN'T KEEN ON TAKING A BATH...

GRITTY SOIL WORKS BEST FOR ALOE VERA PLANTS BECAUSE IT DRAINS WELL.

IF YOU HAVE A SAUCER UNDERNEATH THE POT, ENSURE IT IS EMPTIED FREQUENTLY TO STOP YOUR SUCC FROM SITTING IN A PUDDLE.

NO LONGER *ALOE-NE*

YOU HAVE ONE ALOE VERA, BUT WANT TO MAKE IT TWO. WHAT DO YOU DO? IT'S ACTUALLY VERA EASY ONCE YOU KNOW HOW! (EXCUSE THE PUN...)

PICK YOUR POISON

ALOE VERA CAN POTENTIALLY BE PROPAGATED USING A LEAF, BUT THIS ISN'T VERY RELIABLE. WE SUGGEST USING ANY OFFSETS THE PLANT ALREADY HAS!

FLY THE NEST

ONCE YOUR OFFSET IS BIG ENOUGH, YOU CAN SEPARATE IT FROM THE PARENT PLANT BY FIRST REMOVING DIRT FROM AROUND THE OFFSET.

CUT & SNIP

USE A SHARP KNIFE TO SLICE THE ALOE OFFSET FROM THE PARENT, ENSURING SOME ROOT COMES WITH IT.

PLANT THE PUP

POP THIS OFFSET INTO ANOTHER POT USING A FAST-DRAINING SOIL, AND WAIT ONE WEEK WITHOUT WATERING.

WATER IT

AFTER ONE WEEK HAS PASSED, YOU CAN WATER YOUR PLANT AND LOOK AFTER IT HOW YOU WOULD ANY OTHER ALOE VERA!

ARE YOU PEELING WELL?

YOU WANT TO USE ALOE VERA, A NATURAL MIRACLE WORKER, BUT DON'T KNOW WHERE TO START. IT'S NOT ROCKET SCIENCE, AND YOU DON'T NEED MANY TOOLS FOR THE JOB EITHER!

CUT OFF AN ARM

1. USING A SHARP BLADE, SLICE THROUGH THE BOTTOM OF AN ALOE ARM - CAREFUL NOT TO PRICK YOURSELF.

2. ONCE CHOPPED, YOU'LL SEE A YELLOW SAP OOZE OUT - REMOVE THIS BY LETTING IT DRAIN FOR 1 HOUR.

3. NOW WASH YOUR ALOE ARM UNDER COOL, RUNNING WATER.

YOU CAN NOW BEGIN TO EXTRACT THE GEL.

CHOP OFF THE SHARP EDGES OF THE ALOE ARM FIRST.

GENTLY REMOVE THE SKIN FROM THE ALOE ARM BY PEELING OR SLICING IT OFF.

TAKE YOUR LEAF AND SCOOP OFF ANY ALOE GEL THAT REMAINS.

TRIM ANY YELLOWISH LAYERS THAT REMAIN UNTIL A CLEAR PULP IS REVEALED.

ONE QUICK RINSE, AND YOU'RE READY TO USE YOUR ALOE VERA GEL!

DON'T FORGET

1. TO DRINK WATER.

2. GET SOME SUN.

YOU'RE BASICALLY A
HOUSEPLANT WITH MORE

Complicated

EMOTIONS.

VERA GOOD ADVICE

EVEN THOUGH THIS PLANT REPRESENTS HEALTH, THEY STILL NEED CARE AND ATTENTION TO STAY ALIVE. IF YOU NOTICE ANY OF THESE SIGNS, YOU SHOULD ACT QUICKLY TO SAVE VERA'S LIFE!

NOT DRAINING IT

A DRAINAGE HOLE IS NECESSARY IF YOU DON'T WANT YOUR ALOE VERA TO DIE A SOGGY, FLOPPY DEATH.

NOT WATERING ENOUGH

ALOES DON'T NEED LOADS OF WATER, BUT THEY STILL NEED A TRICKLE NOW AND THEN.

SUNNY SIDE UP

DON'T PUT YOUR ALOE IN DIRECT SUNLIGHT OR IN A DARK, SHADY CUPBOARD. SIMPLE REALLY!

TEMPERATURE CHANGES

ALOE VERA IS VERY SENSITIVE TO TEMPRATURE CHANGES, SO KEEP IT IN A PLACE WHERE A DRAFT OR FLUCTUATION IS AT A MINIMUM.

SOIL ISSUES

THE WRONG KIND OF SOIL CAN UPSET THIS PLANT - MAKE SURE YOU USE FAST-DRAINING SOIL TO PROTECT IT FROM WATERLOGGING!

PESTS

LIKE ALL PLANTS, INSECTS CAN BE THE DOWNFALL FOR THIS SUCCULENT, SO INSPECT IT REGULARLY, AND TAKE ACTION IF YOU NOTICE ANY CREEPY CRAWLIES!

ALOE ISN'T VERY WELL...

YOU WOULDN'T THINK IT'D BE POSSIBLE FOR THIS MIRACLE PLANT TO SUFFER AILMENTS (AFTER ALL, ISN'T IT SUPPOSED TO CURE MOST THINGS?), BUT POOR LITTLE VERA MIGHT BE ON ITS WAY OUT...

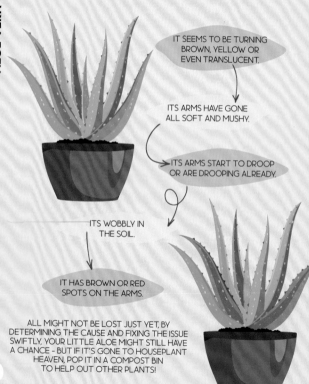

IT SEEMS TO BE TURNING BROWN, YELLOW OR EVEN TRANSLUCENT.

ITS ARMS HAVE GONE ALL SOFT AND MUSHY.

ITS ARMS START TO DROOP OR ARE DROOPING ALREADY.

ITS WOBBLY IN THE SOIL.

IT HAS BROWN OR RED SPOTS ON THE ARMS.

ALL MIGHT NOT BE LOST JUST YET, BY DETERMINING THE CAUSE AND FIXING THE ISSUE SWIFTLY, YOUR LITTLE ALOE MIGHT STILL HAVE A CHANCE - BUT IF IT'S GONE TO HOUSEPLANT HEAVEN, POP IT IN A COMPOST BIN TO HELP OUT OTHER PLANTS!

SHUI THAT WAY

FENG SHUI IS A COMMON PRACTICE THAT INTENDS TO HARMONISE PEOPLE WITH THEIR ENVIRONMENT. SO, EVEN IF YOUR LIFE SEEMS CHAOTIC, YOUR HOME CAN BE A HAVEN FOR RELAXATION AND GOOD VIBES!

TO ATTRACT:

PROTECTION:
MOTHER IN LAW'S TONGUE

AIR PURIFYING:
ARECA PALM

WEALTH AND PROSPERITY:
THE MONEY TREE

LOVE AND HAPPINESS:
LUCKY BAMBOO
(TWO STALKS FOR LOVE,
THREE FOR HAPPINESS!)

RELAXATION:
PHILODENDRON

PACK UP FENGS AND GO A-SHUI

IT IS NOT JUST ABOUT WHICH PLANTS YOU PUT IN YOUR HOME, BUT ALSO WHERE YOU PUT THEM! YOU CAN'T JUST WHACK A PLANT UNDER THE STAIRS AND EXPECT IT TO IMPROVE YOUR LIFE AUTOMATICALLY!

CALLED BAGUA AREAS, THE ENERGY IN DIFFERENT SPACES OF YOUR HOUSE CAN CHANGE THE EFFECTS OF YOUR BELOVED BOTANICALS!

PLACING YOUR PLANTS IN EAST, SOUTHEAST AND SOUTH BAGUA AREAS ARE GREAT FOR OPTIMUM FENG SHUI, DUE TO MAXIMUM SUNLIGHT AND ENERGY EXPOSURE!

THIS IS BECAUSE THE NORTHEAST AND SOUTHWEST AREAS BELONG TO THE EARTH ELEMENT, AND PLACING PLANTS IN THESE SPACES, AS WELL AS THE CENTRE OF THE HOME, CAN WEAKEN THE POSITIVE ENERGIES AROUND THE HOUSE!

HARMONIOUS HYDRANGEA

A FIRM FAVOURITE, THESE BEAUTIFUL FLORAL BALLS CAN BE NOTORIOUSLY HARD TO MAINTAIN, AND HAVE HIGH STANDARDS, MAKING THEM A BIT OF A PRINCESS!

A HEALTHY HYDRANGEA WILL SHOW A LITTLE BIT OF GREEN UNDER THEIR BARKY STEMS, BUT IF YOUR STEMS ARE LOOKING A LITTLE... WELL, DEAD... THIS MAY BE BECAUSE YOU ARE WRONGLY WATERING!

DID YOU KNOW HYDRANGEAS DRINK THROUGH THEIR LEAVES, NOT THEIR STEMS? TO KEEP THESE BEAUTIES ALIVE, SUBMERGE THEM BLOOM-FIRST IN WATER FOR BETWEEN 20 AND 40 MINUTES! BE WARNED - IF YOU LEAVE THEM FOR OVER AN HOUR, YOU MAY DO MORE HARM THAN GOOD!

SOON YOUR HYDRANGEA WILL BE HYDRANG-YAAS!

RAVISHING ROSES

HAS YOUR SIGNIFICANT OTHER GIFTED YOU WITH SOME SAD-LOOKING ROSES, AND YOU WANT TO KNOW HOW TO NURSE THEM BACK TO LIFE? ALL LOVE IS NOT LOST! HERE ARE SOME TIPS AND TRICKS FOR KEEPING YOUR ROSES... ROSY!

ROSES REALLY LIKE WARM WATER, SO MAKE SURE YOU CHANGE THE WATER REGULARLY WITH A WARM REFILL!

PLACE THE ROSES OUT OF DIRECT SUNLIGHT TO KEEP THEM FROM DRYING OUT! IF ROSES BECOME TOO DRY, THE PETALS WILL BECOME WEAK AND BEGIN TO FALL OR BECOME LIMP!

ROSES ARE VERY DELICATE FLOWERS, AND SO NEED TO BE PLACED IN A CLEAN VASE! THE BACTERIA OF DIRTY VASES CAN HAVE YOUR LOWERS LOOKING LIMP AFTER JUST A FEW DAYS!

LUXURIOUS LILIES

WANT TO STOP LILIES LOOKING A LITTLE LIMP?
THOUGH THEY'RE THE MOST POPULAR FLOWER BY
CHOICE FOR FUNERALS, YOU DON'T HAVE TO LET
YOUR CHOPPED FLOWERS KICK THE BUCKET JUST YET!

LILIES REALLY DON'T WANT TO SIT IN THE SAME STAGNAN
WATER TILL THEY REACH THEIR DEMISE, SO DON'T MAKE
THE SAME MISTAKE OF MOST LILY RECIPIENTS - REPLACE
THE WATER OFTEN TO KEEP YOUR LILIES HAPPY.

LILIES ARE WIMPS, ESPECIALLY ONCE CUT, AND THEY DON'T
RESPOND WELL TO PROLONGED HEAT OR SUNLIGHT - TO
GET THE MOST OUT OF YOUR LILIES, STORE THEM IN A
COOL, DARK PLACE. IF THERE IS ENOUGH ROOM IN YOUR
FRIDGE, KEEP THEM THERE OVERNIGHT!!

LILIES HAVE LOTS OF POLLEN, ANY POLLEN FALL CAN
ACTUALLY EAT AWAY AT YOUR PETALS - LIMITING THEIR
LIFESPAN. TRY TO GENTLY PLUCK AWAY ANY PESKY POLLEN
- WITHOUT IT TOUCHING THE PETALS, OF COURSE!

LET'S
root
FOR EACH
OTHER AND
WATCH EACH
OTHER
grow!

SENSATIONAL SUNFLOWERS

SUNFLOWERS LIKE TO DRINK A LOT OF WATER TO STAY ALIVE, SO KEEPING THEM WELL HYDRATED - EVEN WHEN CUT - WILL ALLOW YOUR SUNNIES TO REMAIN... WELL, SUNNY!

REMOVING LEAVES THAT SIT BELOW THE WATERLINE IS A TIP THAT CAN HELP NOT JUST SUNFLOWERS, BUT MOST OTHER FLOWERS, AS THIS CAN MAKE YOUR FLOWERS ROT QUICKER.

ONE TEASPOON OF SUGAR, TWO TABLESPOONS OF LEMON JUICE, AND ONE TABLESPOON OF VINEGAR ADDED TO YOUR SUNFLOWER'S WATER CAN KEEP YOUR PETALS LOOKING VIBRANT, AND CAN POSTPONE DECAY IN THESE HAPPY FLOWERS.

PUT A SMALL SLIT IN THE SECTION OF THE SUNFLOWER'S STEM THAT SITS UNDERWATER, TO REMOVE ANY AIR BUBBLES IN THE STEM THAT COULD STOP AN INTAKE OF WATER.

IF YOUR SUNNIES BEGIN TO DROOP, CUT THEIR STEMS SHORT AND POP THEM IN WARM WATER TO EXTEND THEIR LIFE A LITTLE LONGER!

ASTONISHING ALSTROEMERIA

THESE EXOTIC FLOWERS LOOK LIKE THEY'VE COME STRAIGHT FROM A 70'S DISCO – THAT BEING SAID, YOU WANT YOUR ALSTROMERIA TO BE 'AH, HA, HA, HA, STAYIN' ALIVE' – OR WHATEVER BEE GEE'S SANG...

WHEN YOU FIRST RECEIVE THEM, YOU SHOULD WAIT TILL THE WATER IN YOUR VASE IS AT ROOM TEMPERATURE, AS BOTH COLD AND WARM WATER CAN SHOCK THEM.

MAKE SURE THESE FLOWERS ARE KEPT AWAY FROM TOO MUCH HEAT, COLD DRAFTS AND DIRECT SUNLIGHT, AS THEY CAN EASILY BE DISTURBED BY CHANGES IN TEMPERATURE.

TRIM THE STEMS AT AN ANGLE WHILE THEY ARE UNDERWATER, SO THE STEMS DON'T GAIN TOO MANY AIR BUBBLES AND SO WATER CAN EASILY GO UP THE STEMS TO THE FLOWERS.

DAINTY DAFFODILS

DAFFODILS ARE GREAT... THAT IS TILL YOU TAKE THEM HOME AND THEY FLOP QUICKER THAN A PANCAKE. DON'T WORRY THOUGH – WE'LL HAVE YOUR DAFFS SPRINGING BACK TO LIFE IN NO TIME!

AS SOON AS DAFFODILS ARE INITIALLY CUT, THEY SHOULD BE PLACE IN WARM WATER AND HAVE A FEW HOURS TO REST BEFORE BEING ARRANGED IN A VASE. CUT THE STEMS WHILE THEY ARE UNDERWATE TO AVOID ANY AIR BUBBLES FROM FORMING IN THE STEMS.

WHEN PLACING THEM INTO A VASE, THEY SHOULD BE KEPT SEPARATE FROM ANY OTHER FLOWER VARIETY, AS THE SAP FROM DAFFODIL STEMS IS TOXIC TO OTHER FLOWERS. REPLACE THE VAS WATER EVERY TWO DAYS TO PRESERVE THEM.

TWO TABLESPOONS OF LEMON JUICE, ONE TABLESPOON OF SUGAR AND HALF A TEASPOON OF BLEACH IN THE DAFFODIL'S WATER WILL HELP KEEP THEM BRIGHT AND UPRIGHT FOR LONGER!

DAFFODILS CAN BE TOXIC TO BOTH HUMANS AND PETS, SO BE CAREFUL HANDLING THEM AND KEEP OUT OF REACH OF PETS AND CHILDREN!

CAVALIER CARNATIONS

LOOKING LIKE A SHOWER LOOFA, THESE PUFFY FLOW-
ERS REALLY KNOW HOW TO BLOOM! BUT HOW DO
YOU KEEP THEM LOOKING MORE BEAUTIFUL AND LESS
LIKE AN OLD, SOGGY CABBAGE LEAF?

A BOUQUET OF CARNATIONS IS A SIMPLE YET BEAUTIFUL
GIFT TO RECEIVE. THAT BEING SAID, WE NEED TO KEEP
THEM LOOKING THAT WAY FOR AS LONG AS POSSIBLE!

WHEN PREPARING THESE FLOWERS, YOU SHOULD CHOP
THE STEM DIAGONALLY AND REMOVE ANY LEAVES
THAT WILL SIT BELOW WATER LEVEL -
TO AVOID PREMATURE DEATH.

CARNATIONS ARE QUITE TOUGH, SO SHOULD DO FINE WITHOU
MUCH INTERFERENCE. MAKE SURE THEY'RE KEPT AWAY FROM
DRAFTS AND DIRECT SUNLIGHT, AND CHOP THE STEM SOME
MORE IF THEY'RE LOOKING A LITTLE DULL.

CHARISMATIC CHRYSANTHEMUMS

CHRYSANTHEMUMS ARE FOUND IN NEARLY EVERY BOUQUET OF FLOWERS, AND THAT'S BECAUSE THEY'RE BRIGHT AND VIBRANT. THEY'RE QUITE TOUGH FOR A FLOWER, BUT IN ORDER TO KEEP THEM THIS WAY, YOU SHOULD FOLLOW THESE STEPS:

SNIP THE STEMS DIAGONALLY SO THEY CAN DRINK MORE WATER - THE SHORTER THE STEM, THE MORE WATER THESE FLOWERS WILL TAKE IN.

ENSURE THE BASE WATER IS AT ROOM TEMPERATURE BEFORE ADDING YOUR FLOWERS, AND ADD A FEW DROPS OF BLEACH TO THE MIX TO KEEP BACTERIA AT BAY.

REMOVE ALL THE LEAVES AS THESE CAN TURN YELLOW VERY QUICKLY AND MAKE YOUR BUNCH LOOK HALF-DEAD - EVEN WHEN YOUR FLOWERS ARE STILL HEALTHY!

BEWITCHING BIRD OF PARADISE

THESE EXOTIC FLOWERS LOOK LIKE THEY COULD BE HARD TO HANDLE, BUT WITH THE RIGHT CARE, THE BIRD OF PARADISE CAN LIGHT UP YOUR HOME WITHOUT MUCH EFFORT!

SNIP THE STEM UNDERWATER, IN A DIAGONAL MOTION TO ENSURE IT CAN TAKE IN ENOUGH WATER FOR THE FLOWERS.

KEEP REMOVING ANY DEAD LEAVES AND FLOWER HEADS TO HELP THE REST OF YOUR FLOWERS SURVIVE FOR AS LONG AS POSSIBLE!

REMOVE ANY LEAVES THAT MIGHT SIT BELOW THE WATER'S SURFACE TO STOP THE WATER FROM GOING CLOUDY, BACTERIA FORMING, AND YOUR FLOWERS PREMATURELY DYING OFF.

Flowers

are for tinder dates,

plants

are for soulmates.

TIMELESS TULIPS

HAS SOMEONE WHO LOVES YOU (OR DESPISES YOU AND WANTS TO SEE YOU KILL YOUR FLOWERS) BOUGHT YOU SOME COLORFUL TULIPS? SHOW THEM HOW CAPABLE YOU ARE AT LOOKING AFTER A LIVING THING WITH THESE QUICK HACKS!

SO THERE'S BEEN A LOT OF TALK ABOUT CUTTING STEMS DIAGONALLY, BUT BE WARNED, THIS ISN'T THE CASE FOR TULIPS. TULIPS ACTUALLY LIKE THEIR STEMS TO BE CUT STRAIGHT!

TULIPS ARE SUSCEPTIBLE TO GETTING BUBBLES IN THEIR STEMS THAT CAN CAUSE PREMATURE DROOPING, SO PRICK THE STEM JUST UNDER THE FLOWER HEAD TO ENSURE A GOOD FLOW OF WATER!

IF YOU'RE RUNNING A LITTLE LOW ON FLOWER FOOD, A LITTLE SPRINKLE OF SUGAR SHOULD BE ENOUGH TO KEEP THEM PERKY AND PRETTY TOO!

ICE CAN STOP YOUR TULIPS FROM BLOOMING TOO QUICKLY - SO YOU CAN WATCH THEIR BEAUTY FOR LONGER.

GLORIOUS GLADIOLIS

GLADIOLUS ARE PERFECT FLOWERS FOR WHEN YOU WANT TO BRIGHTEN UP A ROOM, BUT THEY'LL SOON BE GONE IF YOU DON'T CARE FOR THEM PROPERLY...

A WARM ROOM WILL ALLOW YOUR GLADIOLI TO OPEN UP. BUT ONCE OPEN, THESE SHOULD BE SWIFTLY MOVED TO A COOLER SPOT TO KEEP THEM FRESHER FOR LONGER.

REMOVE ANY LEAVES THAT WILL BECOME SUBMERGED WITH WATER, TO PREVENT THEM MAKING THE WATER MURKY AND BACTERIA-FILLED.

IF SOME FLOWERS START LOOKING A LITTLE DULL, IT'S TIME TO REMOVE THOSE PARTY-POOPERS SO YOUR OTHER FLOWERS CAN PROSPER!

SNIP ONLY THE TIP

SOMEONE BOUGHT YOU FLOWERS? AWW. HOW SWEET.
NOW THE NEXT STEP IS TO MAKE SURE THEY LAST
LONGER THAN ONE NIGHT!

TO BEST PREPARE YOUR CUT FLOWERS, USE
SOME SHARP SCISSORS, AND CUT THEM TO SIZE
(TO FIT IN YOUR CLEAN VASE). TRY TO ENSURE
THERE ARE NO JAGGED EDGES - THESE CAN
LEAD TO ROT!

THEN, ONCE THEY ARE ARRANGED HOW YOU
LIKE THEM, FILL THE VASE WITH AROUND 5
INCHES OF WATER, AND LEAVE THE FLOWERS IN A
COOL, DRY PLACE TO DRINK FOR A FEW HOURS,
BEFORE POPPING THEM PRIDE OF PLACE IN
A WARMER SETTING!

TRY TO STORE THEM AWAY IN A COO
OR COLD, SETTING WHEN YOU DON
WANT THEM ON SHOW - THIS WIL
HELP THEM LAST MUCH LONGER!

"Just because you've only got houseplants doesn't mean you don't have the gardening spirit – I look upon myself as an indoor gardener."

- Sara Moss-Wolfe

VASE YOUR RESPONSIBILITIES

WHEN LOOKING AFTER FLOWERS, A LOT OF PEOPLE FALL AT THE FIRST HURDLE! DID YOU KNOW THAT A DIRTY VASE CAN HARBOUR LOADS OF GROSS BACTERIA THAT CAN CUT YOUR FLOWERS' LIVES SHORT?

TO CLEAN YOUR VASE:

1. FILL YOUR VASE ¾ OF THE WAY UP WITH WARM WATER.

2. ADD IN A TABLESPOON OF BAKING POWDE

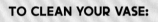

3. ADD A GOOD DASH OF WHITE VINEGAR - YOU SHOULD START TO SEE SOME FIZZING A BUBBLING, WHICH IS EXACTLY WHAT HELPS REMOVE THE RESIDUE FROM INSIDE YOUR VA

THEN RINSE, AND POP YOUR FLOWERS IN AS USUAL!

DON'T BE LAZY - TRY TO CHANGE THE WATI EVERY SO OFTEN, AND CLEAN YOUR VASE BETWEEN CHANGES, TO GIVE YOUR FLOWE THE BEST SHOT AT A LONG AND PROSPEROUS LIFE!

ASPRIN-KLE OF LOVE!

A POPULAR RUMOUR AMONGST BUDDING GARDENERS (SO, MAYBE YOU, MAYBE NOT) IS THAT AN ASPIRIN IS GOOD FOR YOUR PLANTS, ESPECIALLY CUT FLOWERS!

WELL, THE RUMOURS ARE TRUE! CRUSHING AN ASPIRIN INTO THE WATER OF YOUR VASE WILL HELP THE WATER STAY CLEANER AND FREE OF BACTERIA FOR LONGER! THIS IS BECAUSE OF THE SALICYLIC ACID IN THE TABLET.

ASPRIN IS ESPECIALLY GREAT FOR ROSES AS THEY LIKE TO GROW IN ACIDIC SOIL THAT CONTAINS MANY NUTRIENTS. WHEN ADDED TO THE WATER, THE ASPIRIN IN YOUR VASE PARALLELS THE ACID IN THE GROUND THAT THE ROSES WERE USED TO.

HOPEFULLY HORTICULTURE CAN BE HEADACHE-FREE!

WHAT'S THE BIG DILL

BEST HERBS FOR YOUR HOUSE:

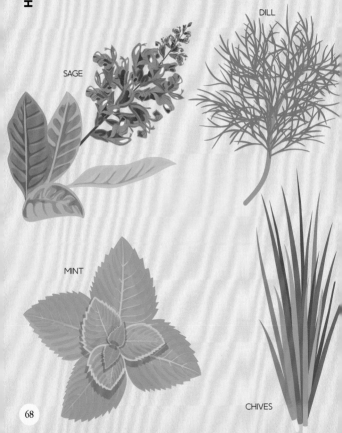

DILL

SAGE

MINT

CHIVES

NOT ONLY ARE HERBS GREAT FOR COOKING WITH, THEY
MAKE YOUR HOUSE SMELL GREAT, AND ARE SURPRISINGLY
EASY TO KEEP (EVEN YOU MIGHT BE ABLE TO
BE A HERB-PARENT!)

HERBS

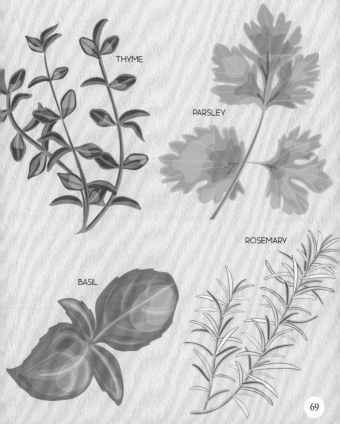

THYME

PARSLEY

ROSEMARY

BASIL

"You can't buy
happiness,
but you can buy
plants,
and that's pretty much
the same thing."
– UNKNOWN AUTHOR

THYME TO GROW

THE BEST THING ABOUT GROWING HERBS INDOORS IS THAT MOST HERBS CAN BE PLANTED ALL YEAR ROUND! HOWEVER, CERTAIN HERBS ARE SUITED TO SURVIVAL IN DIFFERENT CLIMATES:

HARDIER HERBS, SUCH AS ROSEMARY, LAVENDER, THYME AND OREGANO CAN HOLD THEIR OWN IN COOLER TEMPERATURES, AND SO MAY WORK WELL IN WINTER!

LAVENDER

OREGANO

MORE LEAFY HERBS, SUCH AS BASIL, TARRAGON, CHIVES AND CORIANDER DO WELL IN DIRECT SUNLIGHT, AND WILL THRIVE WHEN PLANTED IN SUMMER!

TARRAGON

CORIANDER

HERB YOU HAD GREEN FINGERS

PICK A LOVELY
TERRACOTTA POT

FILL THE POT WITH MOIST
SOIL ¾ OF THE WAY AND
POKE HOLES INTO THE SOIL
FOR YOUR SEEDS.

PLANT YOUR HERB SEEDS
- SIX INCHES APART OR 2-3
SEEDS IN EACH POT.

PAT DOWN THE SOIL GENTLY
TO ENSURE YOUR SEEDS
CAN GROW HAPPILY.

THERE'S NO HASSLE WHEN IT COMES TO POTTING HERBS, CONTRARY TO POPULAR BELIEF. WITH THESE SMALL STEPS, YOU CAN BE ON YOUR WAY TO A PARSLEY PARADISE!

COVER YOUR POTS WITH PLASTIC WRAP - TO STOP YOUR SEEDS FROM DRYING TOO MUCH.

WATER (THE SOIL SHOULD BE MOIST BUT NOT SOGGY).

YOU CAN GROW YOUR HERBS IN JUST ABOUT ANYTHING WHICH HAS A DRAINAGE HOLE - TOILET ROLLS, PLANT POTS OR EVEN LAST NIGHT'S TAKEAWAY TRAY!

TOP TIP:
HERBS NEED PLENTY OF LIGHT - SO APPROXIMATELY 6 HOURS OF DIRECT SUN A DAY CAN DO YOUR HERBS WONDERS!

DO *DRY* THIS AT HOME

IT'S NOT AS SCARY AS IT SEEMS, JUST
FOLLOW THE BELOW STEPS AND YOU'LL BE ON YOUR
WAY TO SEASONING EVERYTHING YOU EAT!

LOW-MOISTURE HERBS SUCH AS SAGE, THYME, BAY LEAVES AND ROSEMA
(TO NAME A FEW) ARE BEST AIR-DRIED. SIMPLY TRIM YOUR FRESH HERBS
AN ANGLE TO AVOID DAMAGING THE REST OF YOUR PLANT.

NOW YOU CAN PREPARE TO BUNDLE YOUR HERB'S BRANCHES TOGETHE
REMEMBER, THE LESS BRANCHES YOU HAVE IN A BUNDLE, THE QUICKE
THEY'LL DRY. 5-10 BRANCHES IS A GOOD QUANTITY TO BEGIN WITH.

FIND A PERFECT SPOT TO HANG YOUR BUNDL
THIS IS IDEALLY A DARK, COOL AND DRY PLAC
LIKE A PANTRY OR UNDER-STAIRS CUPBOARD

HANG YOUR BUNDLES STEM SIDE UP TO
ALLOW YOUR HERBS TO DRY QUICKER AN
FULLY. YOU SHOULD ALLOW AROUND SEV
TO TEN DAYS TO DRY.

ONCE YOUR HERB LEAVES SOUND CRUNCH
WHEN CRUSHED, YOU'RE GOOD TO GO!
SEAL YOUR HERBS IN SEPARATE AIRTIGHT
CONTAINERS TO KEEP THEM FRESH!

"PLANTS ARE LIKE PEOPLE: HEY'RE ALL DIFFERENT AND A LITTLE BIT STRANGE."

– JOHN KEHOE

PALE LEAVES

IF YOUR PLANT'S LEAVES ARE LOOKING A LITTLE PALE AND UNWELL, YOU FIRST NEED TO CHECK IF IT'S JUST A NEW LEAF GROWING OR IF IT'S SOMETHING MORE SINISTER. IF IT'S THE LATTER, DON'T WORRY TOO MUCH, YOUR PLANT CAN BE BROUGHT BACK TO HEALTH!

UNDER-WATERING

IF YOUR SOIL IS DRY, YOUR PLANT COULD BE THIRSTY. WATER IT MORE OFTEN!

TOO MUCH SUN

IF YOUR PLANT IS LEFT IN DIRECT SUNLIGHT, THERE IS A CHANCE THAT IT IS BURNING. MOVE IT OFF THAT WINDOWSILL!

NOT ENOUGH SUN

IF YOUR PLANT IS IN A SHADY CORNER OF YOUR HOME, IT MIGHT BE LONGING FOR A BRIGHTER PLACE.

PEST INFESTATION

GIVE YOUR PLANT A BATH IN SOAP AND WATER - ONLY USE INSECTICIDES IF NECESSARY!

DEAD LEAVES

DOES THE TOP OF YOUR PLANT LOOK AS HEALTHY AS CAN BE, BUT THE BASE LOOKS LIKE IT'S READY TO RETIRE? DYING LEAVES AT THE BOTTOM OF YOUR BELOVED PLANT MIGHT CAUSE YOU TO WORRY, BUT IT COULD BE SOMETHING SIMPLE...

AGING

AS THEY AGE, PLANTS WILL SHED THEIR BOTTOM LEAVES TO ALLOW FOR NEW LEAVES TO TAKE THEIR PLACE. SO IF IT'S A SLOW CHANGE, DON'T WORRY JUST YET.

LIGHT CHANGES

IF THE PLANT HAS RECENTLY MOVED TO ANOTHER SPOT IN YOUR HOME, THIS CAN CAUSE YOUR PLANT TO RAPIDLY LOSE ITS BOTTOM LEAVES.
MOVE IT BACK!

LACK OF WATER

IF YOUR SOIL IS DAMP, CHECK YOUR ROOTS FOR ANYTHING THAT COULD BE STOPPING THEM FROM TAKING IN WATER LIKE ROOT ROT OR SOIL BEING TOO COMPACT.

CRISPY LEAVES

SEEMS LIKE YOU HAVE A SERIOUS CASE OF CRUNCHY LEAF. NOT TO WORRY, THERE'S HOPE FOR YOUR PLANT YET!

HERE COULD BE SOME REASONS:

OVERWATERING

IS THE SOIL WET? THIS CAN CAUSE ROOT ROT, THIS MEANS THAT THE PLANT IS NOT ABLE TO TAKE MOISTURE FROM THE ROOTS TO THE STEMS AND LEAVES. IN THE END, YOUR PLANT IS ESSENTIALLY 'DEHYDRATING' THE LEAVES AND CAUSING BROWN TIPS!

UNDER-WATERING

IS THE SOIL DRY? GIVE IT A DRINK AND INCREASE THE FREQUENCY OF WATERING. OFTEN TIMES, IF YOU LET YOUR HOUSEPLANT'S SOIL GET BONE DRY, ESPECIALLY FOR EXTENDED PERIODS, THE LOWER LEAVES WILL TYPICALLY TURN BROWN AND CRISPY.

TOO LITTLE SPACE

A TOO-SMALL POT MAKES IT HARD FOR YOUR PLANT TO ABSORB NUTRIENTS PROPERLY. RE-POTTING IS BEST DONE WHEN YOUR PLANT IS IN A GROWING PHASE.

TOO MUCH FERTILIZATION

IF YOU OVERFERTILIZE, WHAT HAPPENS IS YOUR PLANT ROOTS WILL BECOME DAMAGED. AND IF YOUR PLANT ROOTS ARE DAMAGED, THEY WON'T BE ABLE TO TAKE WATER UP EFFECTIVELY.

WILTING LEAVES

OVERWATERING

IS THE SOIL WET? OVERWATERED LEAVES WILL HAVE A VERY SOFT, FLOPPY LOOK, BECAUSE THEY'RE WATERLOGGED. CHECK THE SOIL. IF IT'S REALLY WET, THEN OVERWATERING IS THE LIKELY CAUSE. JUST LEAVE YOUR PLANT OUTSIDE TO DRY.

UNDER-WATERING

IS THE SOIL DRY? GIVE IT A DRINK AND INCREASE THE FREQUENCY OF WATERING, BUT STILL STICK TO THE SAME TRICK, ONLY WATER WHEN THE TOP TWO INCHES OF SOIL FEELS DRY!

AGING GROWTH

WILTING ISN'T ALWAYS A SIGN YOUR PLANT IS UNHAPPY, IT PROBABLY JUST MEANS THEY'VE COMPLETED THEIR LIFECYCLE. YOU CAN SNIP OFF THE ODD WILTED LEAF OR FLOWER, IT WILL ENCOURAGE RE-GROWTH.

IF YOUR PLANT'S LEAVES ARE LOOKING A LITTLE WORN AND WILTED, DON'T PANIC JUST YET, THIS COULD BE THE REASON WHY:

TOO LITTLE SUN

IF YOUR PLANT IS NOT GETTING ENOUGH SUN IT WILL WILT. TRY MOVING THE PLANT SOMEWHERE A LITTLE BRIGHTER. DON'T GO STRAIGHT FROM DIRECT SHADE TO A DIRECTLY SUNNY WINDOW.

OUTGROWN ITS POT

YOUR POT MAY NO LONGER BE BIG ENOUGH FOR ITS ROOT SYSTEM. A TOO-SMALL POT MAKES IT HARD FOR YOUR PLANT TO ABSORB NUTRIENTS PROPERLY. RE-POTTING IS BEST DONE WHEN YOUR PLANT IS IN A GROWING PHASE.

AIR TOO DRY

A PLANT THAT'S TOO HOT MAY WILT FROM DRYING OUT TOO QUICKLY. A PLANT THAT'S TOO COLD MAY WILT FROM STRESS. KEEP YOUR PLANTS SOMEWHERE WITH A WARM, EVEN TEMPERATURE.

SQUISHY LEAVES

OVERWATERING

DRAIN THE POT OF WATER AS OVERWATERED LEAVES WILL HAVE A VERY SOFT, SQUISHY LOOK. CHECK THE SOIL, IF IT'S REALLY WET, THEN OVERWATERING IS THE LIKELY CAUSE.

TOO MUCH FERTILIZER

IF YOU OVERFERTILIZE, WHAT HAPPENS IS YOUR PLANT'S ROOTS WILL BECOME DAMAGED, THEREFORE YOUR PLANT WILL NO LONGER GET THE NUTRIENTS IT NEEDS.

FUNGAL DAMAGE

SIGNS THAT YOUR PLANT HAS FUNGAL DAMAGE INCLUDE A CHANGE IN COLOR, SHAPE OR FUNCTION OF THE PLANT. LEAF WILTING IS A TYPICAL SYMPTOM, TREAT WITH A FUNGICIDE TO REVIVE YOUR LITTLE FRIEND.

DOES YOUR PLANT LOOK A LITTLE... WELL, UM...
GROSS? LEAVES TURNING BLACK AND SQUISHY
(AND POSSIBLY A BIT SMELLY TOO)?
THIS COULD BE WHY:

SOIL IS TOO ACIDIC

MEASURED ON A PH SCALE OF 0 TO 14, ACIDIC SOILS
HAVE A PH OF LOWER THAN SEVEN. APPLY PHOSPHATE
FERTILIZER IF NEEDED.

FROST DAMAGE

IF YOUR PLANTS HAVE DROOPY AND/OR DISCOLORED
LEAVES, THEY MAY HAVE SUFFERED FROST DAMAGE.
MOVE THE PLANT AWAY FROM COOL SPOTS
LIKE COLD WINDOWS.

SUNBURN

JUST LIKE YOUR SKIN, THE LEAVES ON YOUR
HOUSEPLANTS WILL CHANGE COLOR IF THEY
SOAK UP TOO MUCH SUN. BUT INSTEAD OF
GOING BRIGHT RED, THEY'LL TURN YELLOW
OR WHITE. MOVE YOUR PLANT TO SHADE
AND GIVE IT A LITTLE MORE WATER.

STICKY LEAVES

STICKY PLANT LEAVES CAN BE UNSIGHTLY WITH HOUSEPLANTS, BUT IT'S NOT ALL THAT UNCOMMON. LET'S SAVE THOSE GUMMY LEAVES WITH THESE TIPS:

DOES YOUR PLANT HAVE STICKY, GUMMY LEAVES?

DON'T THROW IT OUT JUST YET, THIS COULD BE DOWN TO PESKY INSECTS! OBTRUSIVE INSECTS SUCH AS APHIDS, MEALYBUGS AND OTHER HOUSEPLANT PESTS CAN SUCK THE SAP OUT OF PLANTS.

BY USING SOAP (NOT WASHING-UP LIQUID) AND WATER, YOU CAN WASH THE PLANT TO TRY AND REMOVE ALL THE INSECTS.

BUT BE CAREFUL, IF JUST ONE SINGLE INSECT SURVIVES, YOUR PLANT WILL SOON HAVE ANOTHER INFESTATION, AND THEY CAN MOVE ONTO OTHER PLANTS IN YOUR HOME!

"A BEAUTIFUL
PLANT IS
LIKE HAVING
A FRIEND
AROUND
THE HOUSE."

- BETH DITTO

SOIL SABOTEUR

SOMETIMES THE ISSUES YOUR PLANTS ARE FACING ISN'T NECESSARILY DOWN TO YOUR PLANTS, BUT THE SOIL IT SITS IN. IF YOUR SOIL IS STRUGGLING TO HOLD WATER, CHANCES ARE, YOUR PLANT WILL BE IMPACTED.

SOIL IS OLD

IF THE SOIL HAS BEEN USED AND REUSED FOR SOME TIME, IT MIGHT HAVE HAD ITS DAY! SO, OUT WITH THE OLD AND IN WITH THE NEW - BEFORE YOUR PLANT SUFFERS.

SOIL IS TOO COMPACT

IF YOUR SOIL IS PACKED SOLID IN YOUR POT, WATER WON'T BE ABLE TO GET TO THE LOWER LAYERS. TRY REMOVING SOME SOIL AND FLUFFING THE REST OUT GENTLY WITH A SMALL GARDEN FORK (WHILST NOT HARMING THE PLANT'S ROOTS.)

SOIL HAS TOO MUCH PEAT MOS

PEAT MOSS IS A GREAT ADDITION TO SO BUT ONCE IT DRIES OUT, IT STRUGGLES T GET WET AGAIN - MAKING YOUR SOIL UNABSORBENT.

SOIL IS TOO DEHYDRATED

ADD SOME COMPOST TO YOUR POTTED SOIL TO BRING SOME LIFE BACK INTO IT. THIS SHOULD HELP YOUR SOIL REABSORB SOME WATER.

NATURALLY FERTILIZED

BRING YOUR PLANT BACK TO LIFE WITH NATURAL FERTILIZERS! YES, OLD FOOD SCRAPS AND EVEN HAIR CAN HELP YOUR PLANTS THRIVE AT ITS VERY BEST (EVEN IF IT LOOKS HALF DEAD RIGHT NOW)...

JUST SOME NATURAL FERTILIZERS:

- EGGSHELLS
- COFFEE GROUNDS
- GREEN TEA GROUNDS
- BANANA PEELS
- FRESHWATER AQUARIUM WATER
- HAIR

BASICALLY, ANYTHING THAT CAN BE PUT INTO A COMPOST HEAP CAN BE USED TO MAKE YOUR PLANTS PROSPER - MAYBE STAY AWAY FROM THE MANURE THOUGH...

FUNGUS GNATS

FUNGUS GNATS ARE TINY BLACK FLIES THAT FLY AROUND YOUR PRECIOUS PLANTS AND CAUSE HAVOC, WITH THEIR LARVAE FEEDING ON ANY DYING PARTS OF YOUR PLANTS.

FUNGUS GNATS ARE ATTRACTED TO:

- WATERLOGGED PLANTS
- MOULD
- DAMP, WARM ENVIRONMENTS
- BRIGHT LIGHTING

THEY CAN BE CONTROLLED USING HYDROGEN PEROXIDE AND WATER - WHIC IS COMPLETELY SAFE FOR YOUR PLANT

ENSURE THE TOP OF YOUR PLANT'S SOIL IS DRY.

TAKE 1 PART PEROXIDE, 4 PARTS WATER AND MIX.

POUR THE MIXTURE INTO THE PLANT POT UNTIL IT COMES OUT OF THE BASE.

KEEP YOUR PLANT ISOLATED FRON OTHERS FOR 2-3 WEEKS OR UNTIL YOU'RE SURE ALL GNATS HAVE GON

REPEAT WHEN NECESSARY.

PREPARE FOR WINTER

IT'S IMPORTANT TO PREPARE YOUR PLANTS FOR THE WINTER MONTHS, SO THEY CAN EASE INTO THE COLDER WEATHER GRADUALLY AND STAY HEALTHY FOR THE SUMMER!

HERE'S HOW:

REDUCE THE WATER INTAKE FOR DORMANT PLANTS.

MOVE THE PLANT SO IT GETS MORE SUNLIGHT IN THE DARKER MONTHS.

GIVE THEIR LEAVES A CLEAN – SO THEY CAN TAKE IN THE LIGHT.

KEEP THEM WARM BY INSULATING POTS WITH A FABRIC WRAP.

MOVE THEM AWAY FROM DRAFTS AND COLD SPOTS.

CHECK FOR ANY PESTS WHO WANT TO HIDE FROM THE COLD.

TIME FOR A TRIM

IF YOUR PLANTS ARE LOOKING A LITTLE BROWN AND
DULL, IT COULD BE TIME FOR A 'HAIRCUT'. REMOVE ANY
OLD, DEAD STEMS, LEAVES, AND DYING FLOWERS TO
KEEP THE REST OF YOUR PLANT
HEALTHY AND PROSPERING.

TRY TO TRIM YOUR STEMS
BACK TO THE HEALTHY
PART IF POSSIBLE.

DYING OR DEAD LEAVES AND
FLOWERS SHOULD PULL OFF
EASY ENOUGH BUT THERE
COULD BE SMALL SECTIONS
LEFT BEHIND.

THESE SHOULD BE TRIMMED BACK TO MAKE WAY FOR
NEW LEAVES TO GROW AND FLOWERS TO BLOOM.

SOGGY SOLUTIONS

IF YOUR PLANT HAS BEEN WATERED, WATERED, AND WATERED AGAIN, CHANCES ARE IT'S FEELING A BIT SOGGY FOR ITSELF! ALL IS NOT LOST THOUGH, IF YOUR PLANT STILL HAS SIGNS OF LIFE, IT MIGHT BE WORTH TRYING ONE OF THE FOLLOWING SOLUTIONS...

PURGE YOUR PLANT

YOUR PLANT IS A BIT WET BUT HAS NO SIGNS OF STRESS.

POUR OUT ANY EXCESS WATER, AND PURGE YOUR PLANT TILL THE SOIL DRIES OUT A LITTLE.

REPOT

SO YOUR PLANT IS LOOKING A LITTLE WATER DAMAGED NOW- THERE'S STILL HOPE (SOMEWHERE).

BUY A NEW POT AND SOIL, AND LE YOUR PLANT START FRESH. JUST DON'T OVERWATER IT THIS TIME!

"I LOVE YOUR

Roots,

NOT THE

Flower

EVERYBODY SEES!"

- AKILNATHAN LOGESWARAN

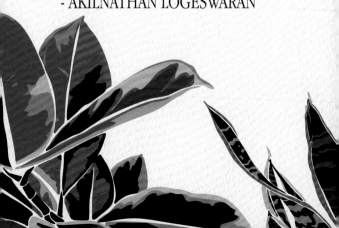

HUMIDITY HEALS

MOST PLANTS LIKE A GOOD HUMID CLIMATE, SO IF YOUR PLANTS ARE LOOKING A LITTLE DOWN IN THE DUMPS, IT MIGHT BE GOOD TO CONSIDER ONE OF THESE CLIMATE TACTICS...

MOVE ROOMS

IF YOUR PLANT IS CURRENTLY RESIDING IN THE LIVING ROOM OR HALLWAY, IT COULD BE A GOOD IDEA TO MOVE IT INTO THE KITCHEN OR BATHROOM FOR THE TIME-BEING.

COVER IT UP

MAKE YOUR OWN DIY ROSE FROM BEAUTY AND THE BEAST BY COVERING YOUR PLANTS WITH A SEE THROUGH GLASS OR CONTAINER. MOST PLANTS RELEASE CARBON MONOXIDE, WHICH IF ISOLATED CAN MAKE AN AREA MORE HUMID!

GREEN HOUSE

IF YOU'RE OUT OF IDEAS AND NONE OF ABOVE ARE WORKING, YOU COULD INV IN A SMALL GREENHOUSE AND HOPE FOR THE BEST.

HOUSEPLANT HEAVEN

YOUR ONCE VOLUMINOUS PLANT IS NOW JUST A DRY
TWIG IN THE SOIL. PERHAPS IT'S TIME TO JUST GIVE UP
AND CALL IT A LESSON LEARNED FOR NEXT TIME. WHY
NOT DISPOSE OF YOUR NOW DEAD PLANT IN ONE OF
THESE USEFUL WAYS?

POP YOUR PLANT INTO A COMPOST
HEAP SO IT CAN LIVE ITS LIFE
THROUGH OTHER PLANTS.

USE THE DECAYING LEAVES TO
CREATE A PIECE OF ART - LIKE A
PAINT COVERED SPONGE.

SPRINKLE OLD LEAVES INTO YOUR
OTHER LESS-DEAD PLANTS SOIL
TO KEEP THEM THRIVING.

USE THE EMPTY PLANT POT AS
AN EXCUSE TO GO BUY
ANOTHER PLANT.

95

"NO OTHER LIFE
IS AS PURE AS
the plants.

IT IS NO WONDER
WE CANNOT
understand
THEM."

- ROBERT BLACK